Genre Realistic F

Essential Question
What jobs need to be done in
a community?

Ben Brings the Mail

by Arlene Block
illustrated by Diane Paterson

Ben will stop here. He has
a big job to do.

There is a lot of mail!

"Hello, Miss Deb," says Ben.
"Here is a letter for you."

The letter makes Miss Deb glad.

Ben says, "Hello, Sam. Here is an ad for you."

The ad will help Sam fix his bike.

"Hello, Meg," says Ben.
"I have a box for you."

The box has a new dress.

Where is Jen? Ben has a letter for Jen.

Jen is not here. Ben will use this box.

8

Ben says, "Hello, Rex."

There is no letter for Rex.
There is no ad or box.
Rex is still glad to see Ben.

Ben did his job. He will head back to get new mail.

Ben will be here again.

Respond to Reading

Retell

Use your own words to retell events in *Ben Brings the Mail.*

Character	Setting	Events

Text Evidence

1. Who is Ben and where does he work? Character, Setting, Events

2. What does Ben give Sam? What does Ben give Meg?

   Character, Setting, Events

3. How can you tell that *Ben Brings the Mail* is realistic fiction? Genre

At the Post Office

Compare Texts
What jobs do people do at the
post office?

Who works here?
How do they help you
send and get mail?

stamps

clerk

sorting clerk

bin

Make Connections

How is a post office worker like Ben in *Ben Brings the Mail*?

Text to Text

Focus on Genre

Realistic Fiction Realistic fiction is a made-up story that could happen in real life. The people and places in the story seem like real people and places.

What to Look for The characters in *Ben Brings the Mail* are like real people. The story happens in a place that seems real. The events could be real.

Your Turn

Plan a realistic fiction story about a job in your community. Use characters, settings, and events that could be real.